# SOMEONE TO LOOK UP TO

Study Notebook

Rebekah Robinson

**BECKON CREATIVE**
PUBLISHING

**BECKON CREATIVE**
GRAPHIC DESIGN

Text and cover design by Beckon Creative

Photographs courtesy of Michael Weavers, Beckon Creative, and iStock
Additional artwork courtesy of Forever.com

Quotation:
**Holy Bible**, New International Version®, NIV® Biblica, www.biblegateway.com
Copyright © 1973, 1978, 1984, 2011 by Biblica, Inc.™ Used by permission of Zondervan.
All rights reserved worldwide. www.zondervan.com The "NIV" and "New International
Version" are trademarks registered in the United States Patent and Trademark Office by
Biblica, Inc.™.

First published in Australia by
Beckon Creative © 2019
Brisbane, Australia
www.beckoncreative.biz/publishing

ISBN: 978-0-6486684-1-1

The author asserts the moral right to be identified as
the author of this work.

**This booklet is a companion work to *Someone to Look Up To*,**
ISBN 978-0-6486684-0-4, by the same author.
A slideshow presentation is also in development.

If you would like to read more by Rebekah Robinson,
see her *Faith Life Art* blog at
https://beckrblog.wordpress.com
and follow her Facebook page
*Rebekah Robinson Author*.

Rebekah's music album *Day In The Sun*
is available on iTunes and Spotify,
or in hard copy from beck@beckoncreative.biz

# Contents

| | | Introduction | 5 |
|---|---|---|---|
| Unit 1 | Chapters 1<br>+ 2 | What Lies Behind Us | 6<br>10 |
| Unit 2 | Chapters 3<br>+ 4 | What Lies Within Us | 14<br>18 |
| Unit 3 | Chapters 5<br>+ 6 | What the Bible Tells Us | 22<br>26 |
| Unit 4 | Chapters 7<br>8<br>+ 9 | What the Pitfalls Are | 32<br>34<br>38 |
| Unit 5 | Chapters 10<br>11<br>+ 12 | What We Could Try | 40<br>42<br>46 |

*This notebook belongs to:*  *Today's date:*

> None of us
> is as smart
> as all of us.
>
> —Ken Blanchard

> Build a team so strong
> that no one can
> point out the leader.
>
> —Unknown

> By this everyone will know
> that you are My disciples:
> if you love one another.
>
> —Jesus Christ, John 13:35 (NIV)

# Introduction

*SOMEONE TO LOOK UP TO* is a book about changing the way we approach leadership in the church. This companion work is designed to help small groups or classes interact with some of its topics. It's a study guide and workbook in one.

In here, you'll find summaries of the main points (I *can* stick to the point when I want to!) and space to journal your musings. I've grouped the chapters into five units, and added questions to facilitate discussion and thought. As the book was written primarily for leaders-in-training, some of them are very confronting questions. This is necessary, if we're going to really engage with the principles rather than just skimming the surface. It's better to ask the hard questions now, than to confront them down the track, underequipped and under the pump, when other people's hearts may be at stake.

If you're facilitating this study on behalf of a group, please allow those present to opt in and out of verbal participation as they feel comfortable or led, rather than forcing confidences (or, conversely, doing all the talking!). Allow each person a chance (but not an obligation) to contribute to the discussion. Go easy, be honest, have fun, be kind. Dream. There's a brainstorm space at the back.

Each unit closes on a positive note, as I pray that this will be an uplifting journey for all who participate. God be with you.

*Rebekah Robinson*
*November, 2019*

# Unit 1

Chapter 1: Because I Said So
Chapter 2: This is the Way We've Always Done It

## What Lies Behind Us

*Let there be love between us.*

### The Author's Thoughts

chapter 1

- "Because I said so" used to be the Given Reason for doing and believing as we were told
- Holding a title was once a trump card of superiority and authority
- Young people are not the only "entitled" ones
- Spiritual authority is godly, but the circle of love may be even godlier
- True leadership will never block the door to God
- God/leaders: respect is a good beginning, but love is the goal
- God's Word is authentic enough to withstand investigation
- Let people belong, with all their doubts and questions and sharp edges; answers aren't as important as empathy
- We are about transforming, not conforming
- All of us should remain teachable
- Complaints can be turned into solution ideas, if there is listening

## Optional Activity

Making time for all to contribute if they wish, go around the room, and as you are comfortable, share with the group where you see yourself fitting into the Body of Christ: your giftings, your roles, your drives. Note these down. (It's okay if you're not sure yet: you still belong in our family.)

---

*"Speech bubble" spaces are provided for you to interact with the author's points on the opposite page. Go nuts. Scribble, rant, doodle, highlight, jot furiously.*

**Your Thoughts** ─────────── because I said so

## Q&A

1. How much stock do you put in "Because I said so"?
   Do you have an example from your own life?
   What do you think was the rationale behind it on that occasion?

2. Authority: How do you view authority in a church setting?

3. Rights: how do you differentiate between
   *feeling* entitled, *acting* entitled, and *being* entitled?
   How do these three things play out in life?

4. In your "ideal church", how would the leadership and the laity relate to one another? Is it relational or positional?
   How would you describe the leader's role?

5. Is there room for diversity in this group? Are we allowed to think differently from one another, or to be at different stages in our spiritual journey? Is there real *listening-to-understand* going on? Can we troubleshoot in proactive ways?

6. How do you regard the authority and integrity of the Bible?
   Is science in opposition to it, or on a path to convergence with it?
   Is it safe in this group to explore doubts without pressure?

7. Are we still learning, and willing to keep on learning?

*Great work so far! Go you! Stand up*

## chapter 2 — The Author's Thoughts

- There are lots of church "ways" that no longer serve us well
- Sometimes *we* wind up serving *them,* and must ask, "Why?"
- You are allowed to own your feelings—but do steer them!
- What works for one may not work for anyone else
- Both the young and the old have wisdom and strength of their own type
- Be wary of painting stereotypes over people

## Q&A

1. Have there been times when you've felt a sense of bondage over activities, methods or systems that you see as *nonessential?* What do you see as *essential?*

2. Are some emotions "ungodly"? Why or why not? Can you express and own your feelings? Do they own you?

3. Have you ever tried recommended practices, only to find them ill-fitting for you? Are there any universal solutions?

4. Do we have subconscious assumptions about people who are not of our age group, not of our experience, or not of our gifting?

*stretch, grab a coffee, and re-engage.*

**Your Thoughts** — this is the way we've always done it

... but wait, there's more!

## Q&A continued ...

5. Can you tell the difference between *Biblical* and *traditional*? How about between *what is appropriate* and *what you prefer*?

6. When was the last time things changed?

Congratulations, you made it to the end of Unit 1! Have a snack!

Before you go ...
seek to understand each other. Mend fences, if necessary.
It's important to speak the truth IN LOVE.
Reassure and affirm one another.

*What Lies Behind Us*

Bring the Lord into the mix.
What prayers arise in your heart as you consider these things?
It's always a loving idea to pray blessing on your leaders,
both absent and present, especially when discussing their role.

Unit 2

Chapter 3: And What's Your Background ...?
Chapter 4: The Big Picture

# What Lies Within Us

## The Author's Thoughts

*chapter 3*

- The four temperaments affect how we relate and minister to each other
- All are valid, and all have strengths, weaknesses, and blind spots
- Each temperament highlights an aspect of God's nature
- You can't major in all four, but you can call in other majors
- "Blanket cures" will produce mixed results
- Leaders and those-who-are-led should not be pitted against each other, but should be a team

## What's in your mix?

| | Choleric | | Sanguine |
|---|---|---|---|
| | Task/goal focussed | | Social |
| | Decisive | | Fun |
| | Extraverted | | Extraverted |
| | Motivated | | Happy-go-lucky |
| | Big Picture operator | | Spontaneous |
| | Achiever | | Supportive |
| | Bossy | | Distractable |
| | Steamroller | | Disorganised |

*Someone to Look Up To* — *Study Notebook*

*What Lies Within Us*

## Optional Activity

Tell us something about what makes your favourite leader so amazing. This can be a church or workplace leader, or any mentor.

---

**Your Thoughts** ...and what's your background ...?

---

*(Circle all that apply)*

Melancholy
- Deep
- Detail-oriented
- Introverted
- Creative
- Planner & sorter
- Empathetic
- Perfectionist
- Oversensitive

Phlegmatic
- Calm & peaceful
- Soothing
- Introverted
- Accepting
- Stable
- Impartial, unfussy
- Lazy
- Flies under the radar

## Q&A

1. Can you see strengths in others that you don't have,
   just as you have strengths they don't have?
   Are you waiting for them to become like you? Is this likely?

2. Are questions welcome here, or are they seen as insubordinate?

3. How can a leader draw upon the gifts of others without
   losing control of the situation? How important is control?

4. Is there a sense of *them and us* between the leaders and the led?
   If so, which direction is it coming from? How can we mitigate it?
   Do you think modern leadership training *underscores*
   or *undercuts* having a Great Divide?

5. Choose two people in the room. In a few words,
   tell each of them one aspect of Jesus that you can see in them.
   *(See that nobody misses out. We all look a little like our Father!)*

*You're halfway through! Have*

*tretch, tell a joke, massage your brain.*

## chapter 4 — The Author's Thoughts

- Every Big Picture is made up of small pictures
- A person's inability to focus on the Big Picture usually requires more compassion than discipline
- Love the lost, and love the found; all souls are valuable
- Restoration is important to Jesus
- The fivefold ministry gifts are prefaced by a description of the *spirit* in which they should operate: humble oneness
- The fivefold ministries help us live out our design as we contribute to the flourishing of the Kingdom
- One leader cannot shoulder all five roles, and their role description ought to be accurate
- Are we focussed on in-house works, external works, or both?
- Churches tend to be like gyms, showrooms or clinics
- Our core business is to win the lost, be the family, and build the Kingdom

## Q&A

1. How do we balance the Big Picture with the Small Pictures that make it up?

2. Are the Lost more important than the Found?
   What happens when the Lost become the Found?
   What happens when the Found become the Lost?

*What Lies Within Us*

**Your Thoughts** — the big picture

... but wait, there's more!

## Q&A continued ...

3. To what degree should we chase wandering sheep?
   How much do they matter to us?

4. *How* do each of the fivefold ministry gifts equip the saints?
   (Apostles, prophets, evangelists, shepherds and teachers)
   Will you release, utilise and back your equipped saints?

5. Which of these gifts does your leader specialise in?
   How can you support him or her in that role?
   How can they support you in yours?

6. Is your church a gym, a showroom, or a clinic? Something else?

7. Do your current projects reflect internal or external work?
   Where do they fit across the spectrum of *winning the lost, being the family, building the Kingdom?*

8. Out of the congregation and its leader, which is fulfilling the vision of the other? Which is therefore truly leading?

*Before you go ...*
*Remember that the thing you're called to do (or start) won't be precisely the same as your neighbour's call. Make room. What has the Lord shown you today, that might prompt prayer?*

*What Lies Within Us*

*Some other prayer suggestions:*
*Pray for each other, for fruitfulness and for sensitivity to the Holy Spirit.*
*Pray for your leaders, for protection and wisdom.*

# Unit 3

Chapter 5: Just Like Jesus Used to Make
Chapter 6: One Plus One Equals Three

## What the Bible Tells Us

### Optional Activity

Imagine what it would have been like to be one of the Twelve. Tell us what you most admire about the way Jesus conducted His ministry while He was physically on Earth.

### The Author's Thoughts

**chapter 5**

- Jesus led a very diverse bunch of disciples
- Jesus humbled Himself, demonstrating servanthood
- Jesus allowed His acolytes to participate in His ministry and even to do it in His absence
- Jesus is okay with slow progress, and more than okay with dependence on Him
- There's a difference between being a supervisor and being a father
- A leader of the Bride is just the Best Man, not the Groom
- Jesus's yoke for us comes with Jesus in it
- Wearing the wrong yoke is not good saint-equipping
- God has an Individual Education Plan for each of us; one size does not fit all
- All is not lost for "unfruitful branches"
- Wounds must not be ignored indefinitely
- Maturity is not the removal of emotions

*What the Bible Tells Us*

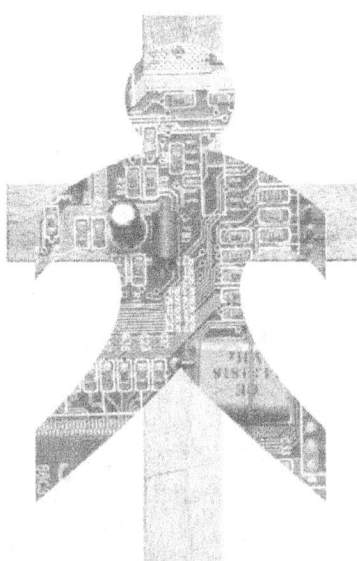

 **Your Thoughts** — just like Jesus used to make

Study Notebook — Someone to Look Up To

## Q&A

1. How do you feel about sharing the load of ministry with a team? How about with congregation members?

2. Does your discipling style involve active teaching? demonstration? empowering? What has worked for *you* as a disciple, and how widely will it will work for others?

3. Can you give people space to *heal* their past, rather than just hurrying them away from it? Are you celebrating their tenacity, as well as their victories? Can you wait with them patiently for breakthrough?

4. Do you see yourself as a supervisor, teacher, or father? What does *discipleship* mean to you?

5. Are you tempted to appropriate the Bride and call her "yours"? Will you encourage people to be yoked to Christ, and not just to you or your church?

*Still awake? Good for you. Shake out your hands. The next round is quite big-*

*What the Bible Tells Us*

crack a smile, do some deep knee bends, enjoy a Coke.
take a deep breath & let's go!

## chapter 6 — The Author's Thoughts

- Leadership is a community activity, and there we find accountability
- Humility, transparency, willingness to grow: **#squadgoals**
- Unity is harmony, not homogeneity
- God gives the church a range of gifts wrapped in humanity; Biblical leadership develops and draws upon them, while unBiblical leadership ignores or squashes them
- Even "unlikely" or "damaged" people have something to contribute, because they contain the Holy Spirit
- Before you "lead someone in the way everlasting" or "see if there is any offensive way in them," first "search them, know their heart, try them, know their anxious thoughts."
- Paul envisaged *everyone* at a meeting having input
- The meeting serves the group, not the group serving the meeting
- Diversity in representation aids diversity in reach
- God often chooses to speak to us and work with us through our peers
- Be generous with relationship

## Your Thoughts

1 + 1 = 3

## Q&A

1. What do you personally find "impressive" in a leader?

2. Which looms largest: the church doing business with God, or doing church business?

3. Are your teams open for diversity?
   Are you willing to love and help-to-save ALL kinds of people?

4. What does "unity" look like to you?

5. What is the pastoral care ratio of *carer:congregant* in your church? Do you know your people well enough to work with their IEP?

6. What level of participation can your congregation expect in your meetings? Is this a Biblical level?

7. Are the square pegs being offered *square* or *round* holes?
   Are they in well-fitted, Jesus-containing yokes?
   Are you training & equipping AND releasing & backing them?

*What the Bible Tells Us*

... but wait, there's more!

## Q&A continued ...

8. Are there any "glass ceilings" in place that prevent competent people from reaching their full ministry potential? If so, why? Could the Parable of the Talents be about development of the *people* God entrusts to us?

*Well done—Unit 3 completed! Thank you for yo*
*(Not to menti*

*Before you go ...*
*Try to remember that these questions are not about finding fault,*
*but about building better models.*

*What the Bible Tells Us*

onesty. It will move you and your ministry forward!
our people!)

> *Some ideas for prayer:*
> *Pray for one another that your leadership work will go*
> *from glory to glory, as you partner with Jesus to grow His people.*

# Unit 4

Chapter 7: Oil Change
Chapter 8: Safe Kitchens
Chapter 9: Eagles, Shields and Pedestals

## What the Pitfalls Are

### The Author's Thoughts

*chapter 7*

- We must hold the Big Picture and Small Pictures in tension
- It's easy to replace "God" with "the things of God," and then again with "the things *I do* for God"
- God is more invested in *us* than in our current vehicles
- Unchurched people have the same basic longings that we do
- We oversell church, then work feverishly to justify it into truth
- The real deal is God, not church

### Q&A

1. What percentage of a healthy Christian's life should be taken up with "church stuff"? Are we clear about what or who we're serving?

2. How are we *really* measuring the success of our church?

*What the Pitfalls Are*

## Optional Activity, part 1

Give each person present a random, useful household item *(peg, paper clip, etc)* and a coin. Have each person give a short sales pitch on the merits of the random item, since it comes with a coin and coin is money. The person voted the most effective or entertaining wins the game.

**Your Thoughts**

oil change

... but wait, there's more!

*Study Notebook*     33     *Someone to Look Up To*

## Q&A continued ...

3. If we are to know people by their fruit, how much slow-growing fruit of the Spirit is enough? Is it even visible to an observer? Is it a lesser fruit we look for? What about negative fruit?

4. Are you asking your people to work super-hard, to the point of bondage, in order to build something that *may or may not* bring people to Christ?

## Optional Activity, part 2

Did you notice parallels between selling the random useful item (which came with a coin), and selling our current modes of doing church (which comes with God)? How do the two ideas compare?

### The Author's Thoughts

chapter 8

- Spiritual abuse is when someone treats you badly and gives a religious justification for it
- A power differential makes it especially damaging
- Abuse is compounded when we victim-blame, minimise, play the "submit" card, entrap, or enculturate the *don't talk/feel/trust/think* rules
- At all times, Jesus wants to be our refuge, but spiritual abuse paints Him as co-perpetrator, placing Him out of reach
- It's up to the leadership to make church safe to serve in
- Forgiveness does not obligate a reissuing of trust
- It takes 2–4 years just to *recover,* and much longer to *eliminate fallout*

*What the Pitfalls Are*

**Your Thoughts** — safe kitchens

*Unit 4*

## Q&A

1. What are the hallmarks of spiritual abuse?
   Can you recognise it when you see it?
   Do you think the church, or your church, takes it seriously?

2. Have you, or someone you know,
   ever been put through spiritual abuse?

3. Have you ever (knowingly or unknowingly)
   spiritually abused another person, or allowed it to happen?

*It's fine to stop the lesson and deal with anything th*
*They require honesty, compassion, perhaps eve*
*With the Holy Spirit's leading, do what can be done in t*
*In Unit 5 we'll talk abo*

*Empathise with the hurt. Affirm one another in love.*
*Ask the Holy Spirit to guide your words and your prayers at this point,*
*remembering that one size does not fit all.*

*Are you ready*

*What the Pitfalls Are*

comes up. These are moments of growth and healing.
repentance, and possibly external, specialised help.
moment; and refer for deeper "surgery" where needed.
preventatives and restoration.

> *If you are unsure of what to pray:*
> *First, listen to each other. Then, listen to God. Pray for each other.*
> *Hear any confessions, and pronounce forgiveness.*

*Let's go on.*

chapter 9 ## The Author's Thoughts

- Leadership is sometimes conducted from a lofty height that has more in common with schools, prisons and asylums than it does with being the family of God
- Isolation breeds risk
- Titles create distance
- Let people love you. Allow yourself to need them.
- Avoid worshipping the Call
- Loyalty is for God alone, but honour and faithfulness are for all
- *Submission* is about uplift, not downsquelch
- Your family and your team remain part of your mission field
- Ministry sacrifices are borne by your family as well as you

## Q&A

1. How do you feel about needing others in the Body of Christ?

2. When you're in conversation with non-leaders, are you letting them have meaningful input? Can you learn from them?

3. How do you personally juggle *what the call requires of you*, and *what it requires of those closest to you*?

*Before you go ...*
*Bring these things before the Lord.*
*You may like to pray for each other again.*

*What the Pitfalls Are*

## Your Thoughts

eagles, shields + pedestals

---

*Some ideas for prayer:*
*Pray for your leaders and their health - that they might prosper*
*physically, mentally, emotionally and spiritually.*

## Unit 5

Chapter 10: And For My Next Trick ...
Chapter 11: An Ounce of Prevention
Chapter 12: Sharing Shoes

## What We Could Try

### chapter 10 — The Author's Thoughts

- We can't apply the old "obey and conform without question" methods to the new "poke it and prove it" generation, and expect them to flourish
- Consultation and client-led solutions are important
- Don't limit your church's expression to a few hand-picked human resources, when God has gifted you with many
- Trust God to speak to people, as surely as He speaks to you; ask people what God's saying; give them representation
- Always explain any hiatus that you impose on someone's ministry; outline a way forward, and honour that agreement
- Train, then equip, then release, then support
- Since *the Church = people,* if you must brand your church, brand it elastically according to the actual people in it
- Consider interactive, non-lecture meetings; don't shout; avoid putting the cart (traditional meetings) before the horse (connecting with God and others)
- Remain teachable, even by people who are "less spiritual" than you; vulnerability and humility are loving strengths
- People want to be connected, seen and heard—and to be afforded the dignity of doing so on their own terms

## Optional Activity

Grab a stack of Post-it notes, and allocate each of the 1 Corinthians 14:26 activities to a square. Talk amongst yourselves about how they might be accomplished, reordered, prioritised. Try the same idea with the spiritual gifts (1 Corinthians 12) and motivational gifts (Romans 12).

**Your Thoughts** ...and for my next trick ...

## Q&A

1. How do you feel about consultative leadership?
   How much weight does a layperson's input/idea/feedback have?
   How do you feel about peer-to-peer ministry? Are *you* a peer?

2. Can you think of any "sacred cows" we could dispense with, in order to help people connect with God more readily during meetings?

3. Is extrabiblical branding something for the benefit of the churched, or the unchurched? How much of a draw do you think it really is, out in the community?

## The Author's Thoughts

chapter 11

- Open communication provides safeguards
- Check that your policies are not hurting or shushing people
- Have a spiritual abuse policy, as a matter of risk management
- Be humble enough to apologise; consider restitution; prize the relationship
- Grace goes with truth; righteousness goes with peace; justice goes with mercy
- Understand the limits of pastoral help, and partner with allied professionals to help your people live in health
- Be careful not to preach mistranslations
- Women are not a minority; they reflect their Maker; and they should neither "man up" nor "woman down"
- Invite your children to be part of your ministry, since they will have to make sacrifices for it either way

## What We Could Try

### Your Thoughts — an ounce of prevention

## Q&A

1. Can people tell you anything, without having you overreact, interrupt or contradict them? Are you safe and trustworthy?

2. Do you have procedures for handling legitimate complaints, and safeguards in place for whistleblowers?

3. Will you fight for your people? Will you leave the ninety-nine and ask the *one* what it will take to bring them home? What could *restitution* look like?

4. Are you as comfortable with your people seeing a psychologist as you are with them seeing a dentist? If not, why not?

5. Do you see women (and their ministries) as equal to men (and theirs)? In what ways does your practice reflect this?

*Phew, that was heavy! ... But of course—these are weighty matters! Take a little time to stand up, move about, have a chocolate, doodle across the page. You're doing great to even address these questions without dismissing them out of hand. Well done. Aaaaand ... once more unto the breach!*

*What We Could Try*

## chapter 12 — The Author's Thoughts

- Walk alongside your people, rather than way out in front; walk a mile in each others' shoes, and talk about it
- Heroism isn't always what you think it is
- God is patient with people's transformation; you can be, too
- Good church leadership is shaped by the fruit of the Spirit
- Are Christians *really* soldiers in an army? Maybe only with special callings, or in focussed bursts
- The disciplined love life works, but it's not very personal
- The Kingdom is not an empire, and we aren't to build one
- Pushing godliness *down* onto people is not the same thing as walking them into godliness *with* you
- Partner with other ministries in your area; understand your locality well, and be invested in it
- You are allowed to receive support from your congregation
- Coach, don't berate
- Don't let people burn out—be mindful of their outside lives
- Let God love you and your family: you are more to Him than role-players; you are not blessed ONLY to bless others

## Q&A

1. Are you able to project the things you're preaching into the wide spectrum of personality types, genders, lifestyles and sets of responsibilities?

2. Do you see yourself as a hero? If so, what kind?

*What We Could Try*

## Your Thoughts — sharing shoes

... but wait, there's more!

## Q&A continued ...

3. How much weight should we give to the "military discipline" approach to Christian life? What are the ways in which Jesus's treatment of us is *like* and *unlike* that of a general?

4. What are some ways we could influence our culture to protect the weak and serve truth, without empire-building?

5. If our programs to *build people up* burn out the staff and volunteers who must keep them afloat, are we working at cross-purposes? (Pun intended!) Is this sustainable?

6. Are you making time in your life to soak in the love of the Lord, or are you postponing this as a "luxury" you'll get to when the needs of others are less pressing? Are *you* sustainable?

*You've done well to make it to the end of the course! May God bless you for your teachability and honesty. The author, and everyone who will serve under you, thanks you for taking the time to properly examine these issues.*

*Keep this booklet somewhere, and perhaps revisit it every couple of years. Jot down new revelations. Never stop learning!*

*And now ... it's time to BRAINSTORM!*
*But first, I strongly suggest that as a group you take the time to pray.*
*Perhaps ask the Lord to hold you together as a group in love,*
*as you wrestle with ideas.*

*What We Could Try*

Ask Him for strategies specifically suited to your situation.
Ask Him for creative ideas and His leading.
Then ... dialogue respectfully and openly with each other,
turn the page and write down the ideas put forward; compare notes!

# BRAIN

*Before you go ... some final suggestions for prayer!*
*Pray for one another and for your leaders.*
*Pray that God will bless and prosper and anoint these ministries.*
*Pray that you will be a blessing to one another for years to come.*

# STORM

### Set any goals?

**S**pecific: what will we change?
**M**easurable: when and how will we know it's worked?
**A**chievable: is it possible?
**R**ealistic: is it sustainable, lining up with our call?
**T**ime-bound: when will we change it? when will we assess the change?

*Pray for yourself! Pray that you will remember these lessons.
Pray that you will always have a sensitivity to the voice of God,
the wit to consult Him in the heat of every moment,
and the instinct to make Him your first refuge.*

www.ingramcontent.com/pod-product-compliance
Lightning Source LLC
Chambersburg PA
CBHW072114290426
44110CB00014B/1913